Castilian Blues

The original *Blues castellano* © Antonio Gamoneda
This edition, copyright © 2021, Quantum Prose, Inc.

Editorial Director
Marta del Pozo

Editorial Advisors
Gregg Harper
John James Steele

Text Designer
Vicente Sánchez

Licensed Art
Detail of "En geometría" © Iván Blanco

Despite the abstract and somewhat calligraphic nature of this work, at Quantum Prose we have found this controlled wash of colors to be loaded with messages: it struck us as an inverted map of the Iberian Peninsula, with a splash of red in its Castilian core, symbolizing the Spanish Civil War. However, this land seems to be now facing right, future forward.

ISBN
978-0-9973014-5-8

Library of Congress Control Number
2021937987

Quantum Prose, Inc.
New York, NY

Castilian Blues
Antonio Gamoneda

Translated from Spanish by
Benito del Pliego & Andrés Fisher

QUANTUM PROSE

Contents

Foreword	9
Blues castellano / Castilian Blues	19

1

Cuestión de instrumento	24
Matter of Instrument	25
Después de veinte años	26
Twenty Years After	27
Tarareando Nazim	30
Humming Nazim	31
Malos recuerdos	32
Bad Memories	33
Caigo sobre unas manos	36
Falling on those Hands	37
Ida y vuelta	38
Back and Forth	39
Sabor a legumbres	40
Legume Flavor	41

Comunicación de males	42
Communication of Misfortunes	43
¿Ocultar esto?	44
Hiding This?	45
Geología	46
Geology	47
Agricultura	48
Agriculture	49
Paisaje	50
Landscape	51

2

Blues del nacimiento	54
Birth Blues	55
Blues para cristianos	56
Blues for Christians	57
Blues del cementerio	58
Cemetery Blues	59
Blues del amo	60
Master's Blues	61
Blues de la casa	62
House Blues	63
Blues del mostrador	64
Counter Blues	65
Blues de las preguntas	66
Questions Blues	67

Blues de la escalera 68
Stairway Blues 69

3

Hablo con mi madre 72
I Speak with My Mother 73

Verano 1966 74
Summer 1966 75

Invierno 76
Winter 77

Visita por la tarde 78
Afternoon Visit 79

El río de los amigos 80
River of Friends 81

Amor 82
Love 83

Tú 84
You 85

Libertad en la cama 86
Freedom in Bed 87

Estar en ti 88
Being in You 89

En la carretera del norte 90
On the North Expressway 91

Un tren sobre la tierra 92
A Train over the Land 93

Siento el agua	96
I Feel the Water	97
La noche hasta caer	98
Night until Falling	99
Después del accidente	102
After the Accident	103
Caigo sobre una silla	104
I Fall on a Chair	105

Foreword

"I feel myself going home": Notes for the English version of a Spanish Blues

A reader familiarized with contemporary poetry does not need to be introduced to Antonio Gamoneda, as he has occupied a central position in the last three decades in Spain. His is not, however, a case of early appreciation of a literary work, as he received little critical attention until the late 80's, when the publication of his collected poetry in a volume titled *Edad* (Age) earned for him the *National Prize for Poetry* in Spain. Later on, three additional awards conferred between 2005 and 2006 strengthened that public and institutional appreciation: the *Prix Européen de Littérature*, *Premio Reina Sofía de Poesía Iberoamericana* and *Premio Cervantes* —the most prestigious literary award in the Spanish Speaking world. This late and slow rise to recognition relates to the particularity, with the uniqueness of Gamoneda's poetics, constantly escaping the mold of his times in a process that set him apart, distinct from the poetry groups and the academic categories that used to define the Spanish literary scene. Meanwhile, as his recent award in México of the *Premio Nacional de Poesía Manuel Acuña* indicates, the prestige of his works has kept on growing internationally.

That recognition of his poetry hangs mostly on the writing initiated with a book published in 1977, *Descripción de la mentira* (Description of a Lie)[1]. As Miguel Casado —a key name in the increase of critical interest in Gamoneda's work— has pointed out, the acquisition of this

---

1] Translated into English by Donald Wellman, Talisman House Publishers, New Jersey, 2013.

highly peculiar poetic voice was also a slow process only fully achieved with the publication of this book.[2] In many senses, *Description of a Lie* set the foundations that support the voice contained in what Gamoneda has written afterwards: *Lápidas* in 1986[3], *Libro del frío* in 1992, *Arden las pérdidas* in 2003, *Cecilia* in 2004, and *Canción errónea*, in 2012.

*

When compared to these books, those that came before (*Sublevación inmóvil*, and *Blues castellano*) seem to belong to a much different cycle, separated by stylistic marks but also by a determining historical factor in Spain: the end of the fascist dictatorial regime of General Francisco Franco in 1975, and the arrival of democracy in 1977. This put an end to almost four decades of an absolutist regime based upon an ideology known as "national catholicism", where a strictly conservative catholic church ruled over all aspects of life, collaborating hand to hand with the dictatorship in the establishment of an iron-handed process of social control. The importance of this fact for Spanish society is difficult to overestimate; in the case of Gamoneda, this historical and sociopolitical change made possible, in one way or another, most of his writing. On one hand, his later poetry, from 1977 onward, has been associated with a poetic recovery of voices and experiences suppressed by Franco's regime. As for *Blues castellano*, the historical change was decisive for a more concrete reason. Written between 1961 and 1966, *Blues castellano* is immersed in a political atmosphere that pushed its author toward the adoption of a dissenting attitude, intolerable for Franco's dictatorship, where political parties were banned and open disagreement was prosecuted, forcing people to operate clandestinely in their attempts to resist and fight the fascist rule. In fact, the 12-year leap between the end of its composition and the publication in 1982 was the result of an interdiction imposed upon it. Franco's censorship mandated that the book be purged of entire poems, quotes, and references antithetical to the dictatorial ideology, something the

---

2] Miguel Casado, "El curso de la edad". Included in Antonio Gamoneda *Esta Luz*, Galaxia Gutemberg, Barcelona, 2004, p. 598.

3] Translated into English by Donald Wellman, University of New Orleans Press, 2009.

poet rejected. But there is an accurate statement contained in the censor's report about *Blues castellano*. Though it dismissed the book claiming a very poor quality[4], when it mentions that the atmosphere of desolation portrayed throughout its pages, without saying it, clearly refers to Spain, it is correct, as the hardships of an oppressed working class are ever present.

*

It is hard not to notice the political nature of the book, but that political substrate is not enough to account for what *Blues castellano* is. Even though it contains important elements of social criticism, *Blues castellano*, according to Miguel Casado, is not a "combat-book"[5]. The poet himself established an important differentiation between *Blues castellano* and the poetic movement known as "poesía social" (social poetry) at least in two fundamental ways. First, Gamoneda has never been a bourgeois intellectual like many prominent poets of his generation, who had to navigate, ironically, the contradiction of their privileged status by distancing themselves from their social class. *Blues castellano* was not an ideological pose, but the poetic manifestation of his personal, intimate experience as a worker and a member of a lower social class suffering the particular oppressive conditions under a fascist dictatorship. Being Antonio Gamoneda, unlike most poets of his time, a self-taught man that truly faced the hardships of the post-civil war period, the fraternity and solidarity within the working class is importantly portrayed in this book, both in its social and its personal aspects, regarding himself and his family.

4] The whole censorship report reads: "Book of very bad verse, of diverse theme and meter. Over it all, stands out a sense of resentment and hatred. There are many quotes of Marx, Lefebre and other Marxists. The general tone of the book is demagogic, because even it's not clearly stated, the atmosphere of desolation it portrays refers to Spain. Moreover, it contains hints of atheism. The book is absolutely worthless, but as there are some passable poems, we've preferred to mark the pages with the poems that should be eliminated. With these amendments, the book is publishable." farogamoneda.wordpress.com. All translations quoted in this introduction are ours unless we indicate otherwise.

5] Miguel Casado, Op.Cit. p. 596.

Second and more importantly, when he wrote *Blues castellano* Gamoneda already had a profound awareness of the fact that poetry is fundamentally about language, even when it is politically charged. In Gamoneda's own words "Poetry is neither social nor poetry if it's not made in a language of a poetic kind."[6] These factors —that root *Blues castellano* simultaneously in personal experience, history, and poetic language— are key to the survival of its appeal beyond the community, language, and times of its conception. These elements also prefigure some traits of the poetics that will gain presence in Gamoneda's work from the 1970's on.

*

Gamoneda has referred to the capacity of poetry to make us "feel" — not simply understand— as the fundamental marker of its effect on the readers. More precisely, he has repeatedly indicated that poetry —defined as "the creation of art objects whose matter is language"[7]— intensifies readers' lives and generates pleasure, regardless of its subject. He believes this occurs even when poetry arises from suffering. These ideas bring light to a fundamental connection between *Blues castellano* and the African-American musical traditions that he also identifies with these roles: "I understood very well indeed that, especially in their origins, blues and spirituals are songs with, at least, a double function, beyond the esthetic one: expressing suffering and seeking solace from it."[8]

Gamoneda described his encounter with this tradition underlining that, along with the musical fascination for figures such as Mahalia Jackson, Sister Rossetta Tharpe, Louis Armstrong and Sara Vaughan, came the comprehension of its poetic features. This contact with what he calls "el cuerpo verbal y musical" (the musical and verbal body)

6] Antonio Gamoneda, "Sobre Nazim Hikmet, los negro spirituals y mi *Blues Castellano*", included in *El cuerpo de los símbolos*. Madrid, Huerga y Fierro, 1997, p. 89.

7] Gamoneda, "Poesía en la perspectiva de la muerte", *El cuerpo de los símbolos*. p. 23.

8] "Sobre Nazim Hikmet...". Op. Cit. p. 92-93.

of these musical genres happened through a language unknown to him, English, that he could *feel*, but not understand. He defines essential features of that "body" as parallelistic repetitions composed according to the tacit law of endless improvisations and variations. With the support of written materials accompanying the recordings, the mediation of impromptu translators, and the French versions published by Marguerite Yourcenar in the anthology *Fleuve profond, sombre rivière*, Gamoneda immersed himself in the blues and gospel, and published the translations of six "Negro Spirituals" in 1961.

*

In an interview Gamoneda recognizes that up until *Description of a Lie*, his writing approach took into account models or references. Undoubtedly the poetic elements of blues and gospel music served as a model or, as he also puts it, a "poetic force" for the book. The mark is evident, especially in the second of its three parts. In some of the compositions, especially in the short ones, such as "Birth Blues" or "Stairway Blues", one can appreciate in all its power the presence of the musical genre they relate to, with its repetition of a few and powerful elements that operate in the linguistic, musical, and rhythmic fields. The soul of the blues is also present in the longer pieces, and in the first and third sections of the book. Poems such as "Master's Blues" or "Cemetery Blues" are rich in rhythm and iteration, but have more space to develop and amplify the atmosphere of despair and desolation common to the blues. The blues, as recognized by the title of the book is, thus, the main force behind these writings:

> "*My daughter was born with a bloodstained face
> and they didn't let me see her.
> My daughter was born with a bloodstained face
> but they took her out of my hands.
> (...)
> Now I ask myself no more
> why one loves a bloodstained face.*" [9]

9] Fragments from "Birth Blues".

> *"It'll be nineteen years*
> *since leaving home and it's cold*
> *and then I get into his and he sets a yellow*
> *light above my head.*
> *And all day long I write sixteen,*
> *and a thousand, and two, and I can't stand it anymore,*
> *and then I go out and it's night time,*
> *and I return home and I can't live."* [10]

But there is another power to which Gamoneda attributed an important role in the origins of the *Blues castellano*: the poetry of Nazim Hikmet (1902-1963). Hikmet, a renowned writer of Turkish origin, had profound communist convictions that cost him many years of imprisonment and are frequently apparent in his writings. Gamoneda saw in him not an ideologue, but a poet who "talked, above all, about the need and the simple forms of hope"[11]. As with the blues and the spirituals, Hikmet's poetry was only available to him in translation, in this case, in French. This circumstance required Gamoneda to make Hikmet's poetry his own by "forcing" the French renderings into versions where he could feel the poetry in his own Castilian Spanish. Here too, certain particular linguistic qualities present in Hikmet are underlined and adopted as important resources in *Blues castellano*.

> I mean, if the metric and rhythm of the thoughts that are there… were not working; if the paradoxical reality and exciting images were not happening; if the expression of suffering were not generating pleasure, I would have respected Nazim very much, but I would not have wasted my time trying to *feel* him in my language [12].

*

10] Fragment from "Master's Blues".
11] Op. Cit. p. 83.
12] Op. Cit. p. 89.

Gamoneda has never made an explicit comparison between the historical circumstances of the African-American people and the Spanish working class at the time the book was written; but this political parallelism, though expressed in literary terms, seems unavoidable. It's important to remember that in its origins the blues lyrics were the cultural product of an oppressed, uneducated, and impoverished minority in the South of the U.S., toiling its way under the cruel rule of Jim Crow laws that persisted for almost a century after the abolishment of slavery. The similarities between these social and political injustices and those committed against the Spanish people in Franco's Spain did not escape other writers. As the African American author Richard Wright (1908-1960) expressed in his book *Pagan Spain* (1957), written after his road trips throughout Spain in the 50's, he was very capable of recognizing oppressive and fascist traits, having grown within them in the South of the U.S.

The evolution of the US Civil Rights Movement and the struggles of the Spanish opposition to Franco are also in step with each other. Landmark historical events of the African-American cause in the 1960's, such as the March on Washington, the Selma to Montgomery March, the Voting Rights Act, or the assassinations of Martin Luther King and Malcolm X, were happening while in Spain other important events were happening: workers organized the first important strikes, university students started their relentless protests, and new trade unions and political parties started to operate, in a clandestine way, inside the country for the first time since the end of the Spanish Civil War in 1939. For those who are aware of these historical trends in both countries, this book may serve as a buckle that tights the analogy between African-Americans and the oppressed and silenced Spanish people. But perhaps there are other contemporary political events, both in the US and in Spain, that allow us to see *Blues castellano* as a living poem, making us feel that the common struggle for dignity, justice, and freedom still reunites our voices and experiences: the

Movimionto 15 M [13], the fight against new forms of authoritarianism, the rise of feminism, pro-migrant and refugee movements, Black Lives Matter... We hope *Blues castellano* could be seen today by the descendants of those that inspired the original book sixty years ago, as a renewed expression of pain, and a song of hope and solace. In that sense, our translation looks to complete a solidarity circle, a fraternal transatlantic embrace.

*

Finally, rendering *Blues castellano* into English makes sense for at least one more reason: the original book is rooted in an "aesthetics of translation". In that sense, it contains a tacit invitation to bring its poetry into other languages. We have already pointed out how the "poetic forces" of Nazim Hikmet and the blues were behind the formation of *Blues castellano*. Both models were explored in languages foreign to Antonio Gamoneda, both were then made his own through a process of translation. The resulting poems were written in a Spanish language transformed in a way that reminds us of the operation that Gamoneda himself saw described, while writing this *Blues castellano*, in Jean Paul Sartre's introduction to Léopold Sédar Senghor's anthology of Black Francophone poets. "Black Orpheus, by Sartre, persuaded me (with the mirror of the French-speaking Black poets from the Antilles and Madagascar) that when the oppressed can only express themselves in the language of the oppressor, that language becomes revolutionary."[14] The apparent simplicity of the vocabulary and the poetic structures; the way in which, nonetheless, the poems are punctuated by estranged, grammatically-defiant expressions; its transformation of the familiar reality into something uncanny; the articulation of a reality inseparable from the language that creates

---

13] The 15-M movement or los indignados started on May 15th of 2011 as a series of protests and demonstrations against the consequences of the world-wide financial crisis that was hitting Spain hard. It opposed the austerity measures applied by the then conservative government meaning cuts in social, educational, and sanitary policies, and related with similar movements across the world. It also meant a critic to the whole democratic system ruled by capitalism and embraced feminism, migrants, LGBT+ and other minorities. It was the origin of the progressive political party Unidas Podemos which nowadays is a part of the coalition government of Spain.

14] Op. Cit. p. 98.

it... all these features are poetic achievements connected to a mother tongue transformed, made foreign, and liberated from oppression through the creative act.

Far from trying to naturalize this poetic language, our own rendition is committed to keeping its foreignness. We have intentionally steered away from producing English versions that normalize expressions not intended to be conventional in the Spanish text. We prefer, in every possible case, being literal rather than altering, with unfounded speculations, Gamoneda's sometimes strange and non-normative wording and syntax. This commitment goes along with certain basic ideas about poetry translation we hold close to, such as when Miguel Casado states that regarding the poem and its rendering into another language "one should inquire what the poem says rather than what the poem *may wish to say*"[15]. This relates to the ideas that Walter Benjamin expresses in his masterpiece *The Task of the Translator*: "the true translation is transparent; it does not cover or obscure the original... This may be achieved mainly by the fidelity in the transposition of the syntax"[16]. Heriberto Yépez, referring to the common failures of many translations of Gertrude Stein's work, round up these ideas boldly: "The worst is the cowardice to literality"[17].

It is important to underline that this is, in effect, an updated version of the book as readers knew it. Antonio Gamoneda, according to his habit of constantly reviewing his writings, has introduced a small number of changes in the poems, some of them of importance. If only for that reason, this bilingual edition of *Blues castellano* will be a novelty also for Spanish readers already familiarized with previous editions.

*

15] Miguel Casado. *La experiencia de lo extranjero*. Círculo de lectores. Barcelona, 2009. p. 107.

16] Walter Benjamin. *Angelus Novus*. Edhasa. Barcelona, 1971. p. 140.

17] Heriberto Yépez. "La diferencia idéntica. Gertrude Stein escribiendo". www.cabrasola.com

Like the original book, but for very different reasons, these translations have been waiting twelve years for the opportunity to be published. We need to thank many people who have helped us bring our dear project to fruition. First and foremost, thanks to Antonio Gamoneda for the trust he placed once more on us, and for his sustained patience and generosity. Thanks also to Amelia Gamoneda for facilitating the communication with the poet. Our gratitude to our friends and colleagues at Appalachian State University who have helped us along the way. First to John Crutchfield and Leon Lewis, who reviewed the few poems published in *Cold Mountain Review* in 2006. Second and foremost to Bruce Dick from the English Department, who carefully and patiently helped us by reviewing the whole manuscript back then; thanks also to Adrienne Erazo, from our Languages, Literatures, and Cultures Department, who has recently done so again, prior to the publication. Thanks finally to the editor, Marta del Pozo, for her surprisingly good memory and her perseverance.

Benito del Pliego & **Andrés Fisher**
Triplett/Chapel Hill, NC
December, 2020

Blues castellano
Castilian Blues

La desgracia de los otros entró en mi carne.
SIMONE WEIL

Others' misfortune entered my flesh.
SIMONE WEIL

1

Cuestión de instrumento

Ustedes saben ya que una sartén
da un sonido a madre por el hierro
y yo sé que una celesta
suena a tierra feliz, pero si ustedes
tienen a su madre en el fregadero,
no toquen, por favor, la celesta.

Yo bien podría. Comprueben
la densidad y transparencia:

"Si pudiera tener su nacimiento
en los ojos la música, sería
en los tuyos. El tiempo sonaría
a tensa oscuridad, a mundo lento".

Lo escribí yo con estas mismas manos
pero no lo escribí con la misma conciencia.

Amo las bolsas de las madres.
Veo:
No hay dignidad sobre la tierra
como el cansancio sin pagar,
el rostro
aplastado,
la desesperación que no habla.

Dejen ustedes. Mi canto está mal hecho
como esta verdad, que está mal hecha.

Hagan ustedes la verdad mejor.
Hablaremos después aunque ya es tarde.

Matter of Instrument

You already know a frying pan
gives an iron mother-like sound
and I know a celesta
sounds like happy land, but if you have
your mother by the sink,
please, don't play the celesta.

I perfectly could. Check out
density and transparence:

"If music could be born
in one's eyes, it would be
in yours. Time would sound
like a tense darkness, like a slow world".

I wrote it with these very hands
but didn't write it with the same consciousness.

I love mothers' bags.
I see:
There's no dignity on earth
like the unpaid fatigue
the squeezed
face,
the speechless despair.

Leave it. My song is badly crafted
like this truth, badly crafted too.

You all craft the truth better.
We'll talk later, though it's already late.

Después de veinte años

Cuando yo tenía catorce años,
me hacían trabajar hasta muy tarde.
Cuando llegaba a casa, me cogía
la cabeza mi madre entre sus manos.

Yo era un muchacho que amaba el sol y la tierra
y los gritos de mis camaradas en el soto
y las hogueras en la noche
y todas las cosas que dan salud y amistad
y hacen crecer el corazón.

A las cinco del día, en el invierno,
mi madre iba hasta el borde de mi cama
y me llamaba por mi nombre
y acariciaba mi rostro hasta despertarme.

Yo salía a la calle y aún no amanecía
y mis ojos parecían endurecerse con el frío.

Esto no es justo, aunque era hermoso
ir por las calles y escuchar mis pasos
y sentir la noche de los que dormían
y comprenderlos como a un solo ser,
como si descansaran de la misma existencia,
todos en el mismo sueño.

Entraba en el trabajo.
                           La oficina
olía mal y daba pena.
                         Luego,
llegaban las mujeres.
                           Se ponían
a fregar en silencio.

Twenty Years After

When I was fourteen,
they made me work until very late.
When I got home, my mother
used to take my head in her hands.

I was a young man that loved the sun and the land,
and the shouting of my comrades in the woods,
and the bonfires at night,
and all things that bring health and friendship,
and make the heart swell.

At five in the morning, in wintertime,
my mother came to my bedside
and called me by my name
caressing my face until I awoke.

I stepped out to the street and it wasn't dawning yet,
and my eyes seemed to harden with the cold.

This is not fair, though it was pretty
going through the streets hearing my steps,
feeling the night of those sleeping,
recognizing them as one whole being,
as if they all were resting from the same existence,
all together in the same dream.

I got to my job.
                The office
smelled and was pitiful.
                         Then
came the women.
                      They started
scrubbing in silence.

Veinte años.
              He sido
escarnecido y olvidado.
Ya no comprendo la noche
ni el canto de los muchachos sobre las praderas.
Y, sin embargo, sé
que algo más grande y más real que yo
hay en mí, va en mis huesos:

Tierra incansable,
                    firma
la paz que sabes.
                  Danos
nuestra existencia a
                    nosotros
                    mismos.

Twenty years.
                I've been
scorned and forgotten.
I don't understand the night anymore
nor the singing of young men on the prairies.
However, I know
there's something bigger and more real
than myself in me, it's in my bones:

Tireless land,
                sign
the peace you know.
                          Give us
our existence to
                      ourselves.

Tarareando Nazim

Tengo ruidos en la nuca, doctor.
Siento el cráneo apretar y crujir,
sobre todo si hay penas. No sé…
Hace ya siete años, doctor,
que en vez de pensamiento tengo un ruido
y una pasta muy triste en la cabeza.

Yo haré lo que me diga; yo tendré
paciencia y confianza. Puede ser.
Yo tomaré las medicinas
para poder pensar en mis amigos.

Pero si lo que ocurre, doctor,
es que tengo algún mal que se produce
a causa del amor
y el pensamiento de la resistencia,
entonces, déjelo; esto no es
más que nuestro sonido natural.
Yo viviré
mejor con este ruido en la cabeza.

Humming Nazim

I've got noises in my nape, doctor.
I feel the skull tighten and crack,
especially if there are blues. I don't know…
For seven years now, doctor,
instead of thought I had a noise
and a very sad paste in my head.

I'll do what you tell me to; I'll have
patience and trust. It may be.
I'll take the medicines
so I can think of my friends.

But if what's going on, doctor,
is I've got an illness produced
by love
and the thought of resistance,
then leave it; this is nothing
but our natural sound.
I'll live
better with this noise in my head.

Malos recuerdos

> *La vergüenza es un sentimiento revolucionario.*
> KARL MARX

Llevo colgados de mi corazón
los ojos de una perra y, más abajo,
una carta de madre campesina.

Cuando yo tenía doce años,
algunos días, al anochecer,
llevábamos al sótano a una perra
sucia y pequeña.

Con un cable le dábamos y luego
con las astillas y los hierros. (Era
así. Era así.
        Ella gemía,
se arrastraba pidiendo, se orinaba,
y nosotros la colgábamos para pegar mejor).

Aquella perra iba con nosotros
a las praderas y los cuestos. Era
veloz y nos amaba.

Cuando yo tenía quince años,
un día, no sé cómo, llegó a mí
un sobre con la carta del soldado.

Le escribía su madre. No recuerdo:
"¿Cuándo vienes? Tu hermana no me habla.
No te puedo mandar ningún dinero..."

Y, en el sobre, doblados, cinco sellos
y papel de fumar para su hijo.
"Tu madre que te quiere".

Bad Memories

> *Shame is a revolutionary feeling.*
> KARL MARX

Hanging from my heart
I carry the eyes of a dog, and downwards,
a letter from a peasant mother.

When I was twelve,
some days, at dusk,
we took a small and dirty dog
to the basement.

We hit her with a wire and then
with sticks and irons. (So it
was. So it was.
                She whined
and dragged begging, she pissed
and we hung her for a better beating).

That dog went along with us
to the prairies and the hills. She was
fast and loved us.

When I was fifteen,
one day, I don't know how, an envelope
with the soldier's letter came to me.

It was from his mother. I don't remember:
"When are you coming? Your sister doesn't talk to me.
I can't send you any money…"

And, folded in the envelope, five stamps
and smoking paper for her son.
"Your mother who loves you".

                    No recuerdo
el nombre de la madre del soldado.

Aquella carta no llegó a su destino:
yo robé al soldado su papel de fumar
y rompí las palabras que decían
el nombre de su madre.

Mi vergüenza es tan grande como mi cuerpo,
pero aunque tuviese el tamaño de la tierra
no podría volver y despegar
el cable de aquel vientre ni enviar
la carta del soldado.

                    I don't remember
the name of the soldier's mother.

That letter didn't reach its destination:
I stole the soldier's smoking paper,
and ripped off the words
saying his mother's name.

My shame is as big as my body,
but even if it were the size of the earth,
I couldn't go back to detach
the wire from that belly nor to mail
the soldier's letter.

Caigo sobre unas manos

Cuando no sabía
aún que yo vivía en unas manos,
ellas pasaban sobre mi rostro y mi corazón.

Yo sentía que la noche era dulce
como una leche silenciosa. Y grande.
Mucho más grande que mi vida.
       Madre:
eran tus manos y la noche juntas.
Por eso aquella oscuridad me amaba.

No lo recuerdo pero está conmigo.
Donde yo existo más, en lo olvidado,
están las manos y la noche.
       A veces,
cuando mi cabeza cuelga sobre la tierra
y ya no puedo más y está vacío
el mundo, alguna vez, sube el olvido
aún al corazón.
       Y me arrodillo
a respirar sobre tus manos.
       Bajo
y tú escondes mi rostro, y soy pequeño,
y tus manos son grandes, y la noche
viene otra vez, viene otra vez.
       Descanso
de ser hombre, descanso de ser hombre.

Falling on those Hands

When I still didn't know
I was living in those hands,
they passed over my face and my heart.

I felt the night was sweet
like silent milk. And big.
Much bigger than my life.
      Mother:
your hands and the night were together.
That's why that darkness loved me.

I don't remember but it's with me.
Hands and night are where I exist the most,
in what's forgotten.
      Sometimes
when my head hangs over the land
and I can't stand it and the world
is empty, sometimes oblivion
still raises to my heart.
      And I kneel
to breathe over your hands.
      I get down
and you hide my face, and I'm small,
and your hands big, and the night
comes again, comes again.
      I rest
from being a man, I rest from being a man.

Ida y vuelta

Has cruzado despacio la ciudad.
Por una vez, tú no vas a trabajar,
ni a comprar una medicina,
ni a entregar una carta:
has salido a la calle para estar en la noche.

Tienes suerte esta vez;
has sabido, esta vez, que se puede vivir
y sentir reunidas tu existencia y la noche,
y que es justo y es bello y es real respirar
en esta libertad oscura hasta las estrellas.

Y, de pronto,
has pensado en tu especie y en tu privación
y en que, todos los días de la vida,
los que no aman la noche nos ocultan
esta paz que hay entre nosotros y las cosas del mundo.

Es entonces
cuando, más que en la noche, tú vives en la cólera
y en el amor también. Y te detienes.

Desandas la ciudad y te reúnes
a otra profundidad también oscura.

Back and Forth

You've slowly crossed the city.
For once, you're not going to work,
nor to buy medicine,
nor to deliver a letter:
you're out in the street to experience the night.

You're lucky this time;
this time you've known one can live
and perceive as one your existence and the night,
and breathing is just and is beautiful and is real
in this freedom dark up to stars.

And, suddenly,
you've thought about your kind and your hardship
and, every day of a life, that
those who don't love the night hide
this peace lying between us and the things of the world.

It's then
when you live, both in rage and love
more than in the night. And you halt.

You walk back the city and become one
with another depth also dark.

Sabor a legumbres

Las legumbres hervidas, golpeadas
a fuego en las cazuelas, espesaron
una parte del agua, retuvieron
otra parte consigo.

Después que estáis sentados a la mesa
los míos de la sangre —cinco— pienso
que es posible que coman en el mundo
muchas gentes, hoy, esto.

Ahora que tenemos sobre la lengua la misma pasta de la tierra,
puedo olvidar mi corazón y resistir las cucharas.

Yo siento
en el silencio machacado
algo maravilloso:
cinco seres humanos
comprender la vida a través del mismo sabor.

Legume Flavor

Boiled legumes, beaten
by the fire in pots, thickened
a part of the water, retained
another part in themselves.

After you, my own kin —five—,
are seated at the table, I think
many people in the world
may eat this today.

Now we have on our tongue the same ground paste,
I can forget my heart and resist the spoons.

I feel
something marvelous
in the crushed silence:
five human beings
understanding life through the same flavor.

Comunicación de males

Mi hija tuvo miedo de mí, y yo que era
el que la amenazaba y ofendía,
sentí al miedo existir.

Debo decirles que yo era injusto:
mi pequeña, mi amor, el ser humano
que se sube a mis brazos y ríe sobre mi corazón,
no había hecho ninguna cosa mala.

No ha sido a causa de mi amor
por lo que sentí el miedo de mi hija,
sino porque aquel miedo estaba en mí
como la luz o el movimiento de la tierra.

Communication of Misfortunes

My daughter got scared of me, and I, who was
threatening and offending her,
felt fear existing.

I should tell you I was unfair:
my baby, my darling, the human being
that climbs to my arms and laughs over my heart,
hasn't done anything wrong.

I have felt my daughter's fear
not because of my love,
but because that fear was in me
like the light or the movement of the earth.

¿Ocultar esto?

> *La conciencia estéril no es más que un momento*
> *[...] de la conciencia desdichada.*
> HENRI LEFEBVRE

Sé que pronto algún rostro golpeado
vendrá a mirarme y abrirá la boca,
y de ella y los ojos fluirá
la pasta roja, la que amo, río
espeso de la tierra, interminable.

Al hombre cuyo oficio y vigilancia
es la vida, feroz como el mercurio,
una bolsa de pena lo acompaña.
Está cansado sobre el propio rastro
como un ave de plomo. Dormiría
sobre todas las cosas: las miserias
y las humillaciones y el olvido.

Pero si cierra el vigilante, cierra
la dentadura sobre la conciencia
y no ve el rostro nunca y el espanto
ya le oprime los ojos, y se oculta
entre los paños de la soledad,
entonces, nada más, se ensucia, llora
y no sale de su caja amarilla.

El hombre cuyo oficio y vigilancia
es la vida ¿qué hará, cómo podría
subirse encima de la enfermedad,
comprender y luchar?
                    Bajé los ojos
ante el mundo. Cubrí con una sombra
mi vergüenza y mi pena. Me dispuse
a una fraternidad sin esperanza.

Hiding This?

> *The sterile conscience is no more than a moment*
> *[...] of the unhappy conscience.*
> HENRI LEFEBVRE

I know some beaten face
will soon come to stare at me, and it will open his mouth,
and the red paste will flow out of it and out of his eyes;
the paste I love, the thick,
endless river of earth.

A bag of sorrows accompanies
the man, fierce as mercury,
whose job and vigilance is life.
He's tired on his own track
like a bird of lead. He'd sleep
over all things: miseries,
and humiliations, and oblivion.

But if the watchman locks up, locks up
his teeth over the conscience,
and he never sees the face, and terror
already squeezes his eyes and he hides
behind the clothes of solitude,
then, no more, he gets himself dirty, weeps
and doesn't step out of his yellow box.

What will he do, the man whose job and vigilance
is life? How would he
climb on top of the disease
and understand and fight?
                               I lowered my eyes
in front of the world. I wrapped my shame and sorrow
with a shadow. I got ready
for a hopeless brotherhood.

Geología

Algunas veces salgo hacia las montañas
a mirar a lo lejos.

Piso unas lomas donde tierra vieja
se pone hermosa con el sol y veo
subir la sombra por los cuestos.
                                      Ando
mucho tiempo en silencio.

Pero hay días que ando por estas lomas,
y miro hacia las montañas,
y ni allí hay libertad.

Y me vuelvo. Yo sé bien que es inútil
buscarla como a una llave perdida,
y que también es inútil
mirar al fondo de mi corazón.

Geology

Sometimes I go out to the mountains
to look yonder.

I step on hills where old ground
turns beautiful with the sun and I see
the shade raising on the slopes.
                                        I walk
for a long time in silence.

But there are days I walk these hills,
and I look at the mountains,
and there's no freedom even there.

And I return. I know well it's useless
to seek freedom like a lost key,
as well it's useless
to look at the bottom of my heart.

Agricultura

Qué valdría sin pisadas humanas
esta pobreza que hace crujir la luz.
Qué sería la belleza violenta
del secano sin el corazón cansado
que piensa en él: tierra roída
y mala soledad frente al acero
mural de las montañas.

Mirad, es bello y es verdad: arriba,
el cardo blanco y el centeno, ciegos,
vibran junto a los pájaros, y luego
baja la tierra sobre sombras rojas
hasta el poco de agua y los negrillos.

Baja roída por el sol, quemada
por el hielo como el rostro humano
quieto y tajado de dolor, que pasa,
mil veces pasa por la tierra, duro,
con la herramienta y el caballo viejo,
seco como su amor, mil veces pasa,
toda la vida mientras dura el día.

Agriculture

Without human steps, how much would
this poverty that makes light crack be worth.
What would the violent beauty of the dry land
be without the tired heart
that thinks about it: gnawed soil,
and bad loneliness against the mural
steel of the mountains.

Look, it's beautiful and true: up there,
the white thistle and the rye blindly
vibrate with the birds, and then
the ground lowers over red shadows,
toward the bit of water and the elms.

And it comes down gnawed by the sun, burnt
by the ice like a human face,
that walks by, motionless and cut by pain,
a thousand times it goes by the land, hard,
with its tool and old horse,
dry as its love, a thousand times,
a whole life goes by while the day lasts.

Paisaje

Vi
montes sin una flor, lápidas rojas,
pueblos
vacíos.
Y la sombra que baja. Pero hierve
la luz en los espinos. No comprendo. Sólo
veo belleza.
         Desconfío.

Landscape

I saw
hills without a flower, red gravestones,
empty
towns.
And the lowering shadow. But the light
boils in the hawthorns. I don't understand. I only
see beauty.
        I distrust.

Blues del nacimiento

Nació mi hija con el rostro ensangrentado
y no me la dejaron ver despacio.
Nació mi hija con el rostro ensangrentado
pero me la quitaron de las manos.

Mi hija ya va a hacer tres años
y habla conmigo y ve mi rostro.
Mi hija ya va a hacer tres años
y canta y piensa. Pero ve mi rostro.

Yo ahora ya no me pregunto
por qué se ama a un rostro ensangrentado.

Birth Blues

My daughter was born with a bloodstained face
and they didn't let me see her.
My daughter was born with a bloodstained face
but they took her out of my hands.

My daughter is about to turn three
and speaks with me and sees my face.
My daughter is about to turn three
and sings and thinks. But sees my face.

Now I ask myself no more
why one loves a bloodstained face.

Blues para cristianos

Antes algunos hombres se sentaban a fumar
y a mirar la tierra despacio.
Antes muchos hombres se sentaban a fumar
y poco a poco comprendían la tierra.
Ahora no se puede fumar cuando viene la noche.
Ahora ya no queda tabaco ni esperanza.

Ya han debido de pasar el cielo y la tierra
y todas las casas están vacías.
Han debido de pasar el cielo y la tierra
porque todas las casas están vacías.
La madre ya no quiere volver a sus cazuelas.
Aquí toda la gente está muy triste.

Ahora vendrá Dios con su madero.
Dicen que viene Jesucristo con su madero.
Bien, que venga con su madero.

Cuando venga Jesucristo con su madero,
vamos a verle la chaqueta vieja.
Cuando venga Jesucristo a vivir con nosotros,
habrá que verle el corazón cansado.

Aquí ya no hay otra majestad que el dolor.
Sí, buen amigo, ya no hay nada más en la tierra.

Blues for Christians

Before, some men sat down to smoke
and to slowly watch the land.
Before, many men sat down to smoke
and slowly came to understand the land.
Now one cannot smoke when night comes.
Now there is neither tobacco nor hope.

The sky and the land must have already passed
and all the houses are empty.
The sky and the land must have passed
because all the houses are empty.
Mothers don't want to return to their pots and pans.
All the people here are very sad.

Now God will come with his cross.
It's said that Jesus is coming with his cross.
All right, let him come with his cross.

When Jesus comes with his cross,
we are going to see his old jacket.
When Jesus comes to live with us,
we'll have to see his tired heart.

Here there is no other majesty but pain.
Yes, my friend, there is nothing else on Earth.

Blues del cementerio

Conozco un pueblo —no lo olvidaré—
que tiene un cementerio demasiado grande.
Hay en mi tierra un pueblo sin ventura
porque el cementerio es demasiado grande.
Sólo hay cuarenta almas en el pueblo.
No sé para qué tanto cementerio.

Cierto año la gente empezó a irse
y en muchas casas no quedaba nadie.
El año que la gente empezó a irse
en muchas casas no quedaba nadie.
Se llevaban los hijos y las camas.
Mataban a los animales sin mirarlos.

El cementerio ya no tiene puertas
y allí entran y salen las gallinas.
El cementerio ya no tiene puertas
y salen al camino las ortigas.
Parece que saliera el cementerio
a los huertos y a las calles vacías.

Conozco un pueblo. No lo olvidaré.
No olvidaré a mi pueblo y su luz desventurada.

¡Qué mala cosa es haber hecho
un cementerio demasiado grande!

Cemetery Blues

I know a town —I won't forget it—
whose cemetery is too large.
In my country there's an unfortunate town
because the cemetery is too large.
There are only forty souls in town.
I don't know why such a large cemetery.

One year, people started to leave,
and in many houses no one remained.
The year people started to leave,
in many houses no one remained.
They took their children and their beds.
They slaughtered the animals without looking at them.

The cemetery has no gates anymore,
and the chickens go in and out.
The cemetery has no gates anymore,
and nettles are taking over the road.
It looks like the cemetery is taking over
the orchards and the empty streets.

I know a town. I won't forget it.
I won't forget my town and its unfortunate light.

How terrible to have made
a cemetery way too large!

Blues del amo

Va a hacer diecinueve años
que trabajo para un amo.
Hace diecinueve años que me da la comida
y todavía no he visto su rostro.

No he visto al amo en diecinueve años
pero todos los días me veo a mí mismo
y ya voy sabiendo poco a poco
cómo es el rostro de mi amo.

Va a hacer diecinueve años
que salgo de mi casa y hace frío
y luego entro en la suya
y me pone una luz amarilla encima de la cabeza.
Y todo el día escribo dieciséis
y mil y dos y ya no puedo más.
Y luego salgo al aire y es de noche
y vuelvo a casa y no puedo vivir.

Cuando vea a mi amo le preguntaré
lo que son mil y dieciséis
y por qué me pone una luz amarilla encima de la cabeza.

Cuando esté un día delante de mi amo,
veré su rostro, miraré en su rostro
hasta borrarlo de él y de mí mismo.

Master's Blues

It'll be nineteen years
working for a master.
Nineteen years since he's been giving me my food
and I haven't yet seen his face.

I haven't seen my master in nineteen years
but every day I see myself
and slowly I'm beginning to know
what my master's face is like.

It'll be nineteen years
since leaving home and it's cold
and then I get into his
and he sets a yellow light above my head.
And all day long I write sixteen,
and a thousand, and two, and I can't stand it anymore.
And then I go out and it's night time,
and I return home and I can't live.

When I see my master I'll ask him
what a thousand and sixteen are,
and why he sets a yellow light above my head.

Someday, standing before my master,
I'll see his face, I'll look into his face
erasing it from him and from myself.

Blues de la casa

En mi casa están vacías las paredes
y yo sufro mirando la cal fría.
Mi casa tiene puertas y ventanas:
no puedo soportar tanto agujero.

Aquí vive mi madre con sus lentes.
Aquí está mi mujer con sus cabellos.
Aquí viven mis hijas con sus ojos.
¿Por qué sufro mirando las paredes?

El mundo es grande. Dentro de una casa
no cabrá nunca. El mundo es grande.
Dentro de una casa (el mundo es grande)
no es bueno que haya tanto sufrimiento.

House Blues

In my house the walls are empty
and it hurts to look at the cold lime.
My house has doors and windows:
I can't stand so many holes.

Here lives my mother with her glasses.
Here's my wife with her hair.
Here live my daughters with their eyes.
Why does it hurt to look at the walls?

The world is big. It will never fit
inside a house. The world is big.
Inside a house (the world is big)
so much suffering it's not good.

Blues del mostrador

Llegó con el papel entre las manos
y me miró con sus ojos cansados.
Llegó con el papel y con sus manos
y yo sentí su mirada en mi vida.

Cuando venga otro día con sus manos
y su papel a mirarme en silencio,
espero comprender por qué me mira,
por qué es viejo y por qué pesan
en mi corazón sus ojos cansados.

Counter Blues

He arrived with the paper in his hands
and looked at me with tired eyes.
He arrived with the paper and with his hands
and I felt his gaze in my life.

Another day, when he comes with his hands
and his paper to look at me in silence,
I hope to understand why he stares at me,
why he's old and why his tired eyes
weigh heavily on my heart.

Blues de las preguntas

Hace tiempo que estoy entristecido
porque mis palabras no entran en tu corazón.
Muchos días estoy entristecido
porque tu silencio entra en mi corazón.

Hay veces que estoy triste a tu lado
porque tú sólo me amas con amor.
Muchos días estoy triste a tu lado
porque no me amas con amistad.

Todos los hombres aman mucho la libertad.
¿Sabes tú lo que es vivir ante una puerta cerrada?

Yo amo la libertad y te amo a ti.
¿Sabes tú lo que es vivir ante un rostro cerrado?

Questions Blues

For a while I've had the blues
because my words don't enter your heart.
Many days I've had the blues
because your silence enters my heart.

There are times I feel blue at your side
because you only love me with love.
Many days I feel blue at your side
because you don't love me with friendship.

All men love freedom so much.
Do you know how it is to live in front of a closed door?

I love freedom and I love you.
Do you know how it is to live in front of a closed face?

Blues de la escalera

Por la escalera sube una mujer
con un caldero lleno de penas.
Por la escalera sube una mujer
con el caldero de las penas.

Encontré a una mujer en la escalera
y ella bajó sus ojos ante mí.

Encontré la mujer con el caldero.
Ya nunca tendré paz en la escalera.

Stairway Blues

A woman climbs the stairs
with a boiler full of sorrows.
The woman climbs the stairs
with the boiler of sorrows.

I stumbled upon a woman on the stairs
and she lowered her eyes when she saw me.

I stumbled upon the woman with the boiler.
I'll never be at peace on the stairs.

Hablo con mi madre

Mamá: ahora eres silenciosa como la ropa
del que no está con nosotros.
Te miro el borde blanco de los párpados
y no puedo pensar.

Mamá: quiero olvidar todas las cosas
en el fondo de una respiración que canta.
Pasa tus manos grandes por mi nuca
todos los días para que no vuelva
la soledad.

Yo sé que en cada rostro se ve el mundo.
No busques más en las paredes, madre.
Mira despacio el rostro que tú amas:
mira mi rostro en cada rostro humano.

He sentido tus manos.
Perdido en el fondo de los seres humanos te he sentido
como tú sentías mis manos antes de nacer.

Mamá, no vuelvas más a ocultarme la tierra.
Ésta es mi condición.
                        Y mi esperanza.

I Speak with My Mother

Mom, now you're quiet like clothing
of he who's not with us.
I look at the white edge of your eyelids
and I can't think.

Mom, I want to forget everything
at the bottom of a singing breath.
Pass your big hands over my nape
every day to avoid the return
of solitude.

I know the world is seen in each face.
Don't search in the walls anymore, mother.
Look slowly at the face you love:
see my face in every human face.

I've felt your hands.
Lost at the bottom of human beings, I've felt you
as you felt my hands before I was born.

Mom, don't hide the ground from me anymore.
Such is my condition.
                        And my hope.

Verano 1966

Cuando me extiendo junto al mar,
existe el agua y su palpitación
y un cielo azul cuya profundidad
es demasiado grande para mí.

Sentir el mar, su lentitud viviente,
es la magnificencia y el olvido,
pero sentir la vida de los camaradas
es ser el camarada de uno mismo.

El cielo inmóvil tiene su razón, lo sé,
pero la razón que hay en nosotros
existirá aun cuando ese cielo
haya sido borrado por el viento y el frío.

Summer 1966

When I lay down beside the sea,
the water and its beating exist
and a blue sky whose depth
is too big for me.

To feel the sea, its living slowness,
is magnificence and oblivion,
but to feel the comrades' life
is to be one's own comrade.

The motionless sky has its reason, I know,
but the reason within us
will exist even when this sky
has been erased by the wind and cold.

Invierno

La nieve cruje como pan caliente
y la luz es limpia como la mirada de algunos seres humanos,
y yo pienso en el pan y en las miradas
mientras camino sobre la nieve.

Hoy es domingo y me parece que la mañana no está únicamente
                                                                                                       sobre la tierra;
que la mañana se ha posado suavemente en mi vida.

He visto el río, como acero oscuro
bajando entre la nieve.
Y el duro espino llameando; el duro,
agrio fruto de enero.
Y el robledal, sobre tierra abrasada,
resistiendo en silencio.

Hoy, domingo, la vegetación del invierno,
la nieve tierna y la luz liberada,
se parecen a una realidad, aún sin nombre, que estoy esperando,
que necesito y que amo.

Winter

Snow crunches like warm bread
and the light is clean like the gaze of certain humans,
and I think about the bread and the gazes
while I walk on the snow.

Today is Sunday and it seems the morning is not only over the land;
the morning has settled smoothly on my life.

I see the river, like dark steel
running down between the snow.
I see the hard hawthorn blazing; the hard,
bitter January fruit.
And oak wood, on the scorched land,
resisting in silence.

Today, Sunday, the winter vegetation,
the tender snow, and the freed land,
seem a reality, still nameless, that I'm awaiting,
that I need, and I love.

Visita por la tarde

Entré en la casa y me quité el abrigo
para que mis amigos no supieran
cuanto frío tenían, pero ellos
dijeron: "Ven, entra a la cocina".
Y la madre hizo fuego para mí.

No he podido tener nunca mi fiesta
en paz como aquel día:
el vino en la madera, la mirada
de los niños, las palabras,
el resplandor del fuego.

Cuando llegó la noche, la mujer
sacó las manos del agua
y separó los cabellos esparcidos
sobre el rostro cansado.
      Y vi el rostro.
Rostro cansado: amor.
      Y sonreía.

Afternoon Visit

I stepped into the house and took off my coat
so my friends wouldn't realize
how cold they were, but they
said: "Come on into the kitchen".
And the mother lit a fire for me.

I've never been able to have my party
in peace like that day:
wine in the wood; children's
gaze; words;
fire's blaze…

When the night came, the woman
took her hands out of the water
and removed the scattered hair
from her tired face.
                    And I saw her face.
Tired face: love.
              And she was smiling.

El río de los amigos

Hoy anduve la orilla del Bernesga.
En otro tiempo, por aquí, nosotros
fuimos lejos, amigos.

De cara al cielo, sobre la humedad,
me tendí solo y me cubrían
el silencio y la yerba.

Sentí crecer mi corazón, girar la tierra,
descender el río.

Bajó la sombra y levanté las manos
para ponerlas sobre las cortezas
ásperas y frescas de los álamos.
Era la hora de volver. Había
aquel mismo silencio.

Nosotros pisábamos la tierra pensando
y la misma luz envolvía al regreso
el viejo tronco de los árboles
y el rostro de los amigos.

River of Friends

Today I walked the Bernesga shore.
In other times, my friends,
around here, we went afar.

Facing the sky, over the moisture,
I laid down alone and silence and grass
covered me.

I felt my heart growing, the land turning,
the river descending.

The shadow came down and I raised my hands
to place them on the rough and cool
bark of the poplars.
It was time to go back. There was
that same silence.

We stepped on the land thinking,
and on the way back the same light wrapped around
the old tree trunks
and the faces of the friends.

Amor

Mi manera de amarte es sencilla:
te aprieto a mí
como si hubiera un poco de justicia en mi corazón
y yo te la pudiese dar con el cuerpo.

Cuando revuelvo tus cabellos
algo hermoso se forma entre mis manos.

Y casi no sé más. Yo sólo aspiro
a estar contigo en paz, y a estar en paz
con un deber desconocido
que a veces pesa también en mi corazón.

Love

My way of loving you is simple:
I hold you tight
as if there were a bit of justice in my heart
and I could give it to you with my body.

When I mess up your hair
something pretty is formed in my hands.

And I barely know anymore. I only wish
to be in peace with you, and to be in peace
with an unknown duty
that sometimes weighs heavily in my heart.

Tú

Caer en un rostro, existir
con su respiración y con su boca...

Cuando tú estabas en peligro,
tú gritaste, mas fue
en la garganta de otro ser humano.
Se levantó tu cuerpo
y fue en los brazos de otro ser humano.

Entonces comprendiste.

Y tu necesidad y tus deseos
no fueron ya como antes. Tú
ya no ves signos. Ahora desprecias
todas las dudas y tu pensamiento
no es espejo abatido. Es voluntad de amor,
y conducta, y destino, y existencia.

You

Falling on a face, to exist
with its breath and its mouth…

You cried when you were
in danger, but it was
in the throat of another human.
Your body raised
and it was in the arms of another human.

Then you understood.

And your need and your desires
were never as before. You
don't see signs anymore. Now you despise
all doubts and your thought
is not a downhearted mirror. It is will for love,
and conduct, and fate, and existence.

Libertad en la cama

Todos los días salgo de la cama
y digo adiós a mi compañera.
Sucede entonces
que encuentro los pantalones
y pierdo la libertad.

Cuando llega la noche, otra vez
vuelvo a la cama y duermo.

A veces sueño que me llevan con las manos atadas,
pero entonces me despierto y siento la oscuridad,
y, con el mismo valor,
el cuerpo de mi mujer y el mío.

Freedom in Bed

Every day I get out of bed
and say goodbye to my partner.
Then it happens
I find my pants
and lose my freedom.

When the night comes,
I return to bed and sleep again.

Sometimes I dream I'm taken away with my hands tied,
but then I awake and feel the darkness,
and, with the same worth,
my wife's body and mine.

Estar en ti

Yo no entro en ti para que tú te pierdas
bajo la fuerza de mi amor;
yo no entro en ti para perderme
en tu existencia ni en la mía;
yo te amo y entro a tu corazón
para vivir con tu naturaleza,
para que tú te extiendas en mi vida.

Ni tú ni yo, ni tú ni yo.
Ni tus cabellos esparcidos aunque los amo tanto.
Sólo esta oscura compañía.
                            Ahora
siento la libertad.
                    Esparce
tus cabellos.
            Esparce tus cabellos.

Being in You

I don't enter you for you to get lost
under the strength of my love;
I don't enter you for me to get lost
in your existence nor in mine;
I love you and enter your heart
to live with your nature,
for you to stretch out in my life.

Neither you nor me, neither you nor me.
Nor your scattered hair, even though I love it dearly.
Just this dark company.
      Now
I feel freedom.
    Scatter
your hair.
    Scatter your hair.

En la carretera del norte

Por la carretera del norte
hay luz sobre los cuestos.
                      Ana, Amelia,
venid conmigo a recibir la luz.

En mi mano izquierda tengo la mano de Amelia
y en la derecha la de Ana.
Los tres sentimos nuestra vida y la luz.
Los tres sentimos nuestras manos y la luz.
Los tres sentimos la luz,
el silencio y las manos.

Hubo un día en que anduve por la tierra sin nadie.
Aún caía el sol sobre el cuesto amarillo
pero la soledad cegaba la luz.

Aunque haya sol sobre la tierra, amigos,
no vayáis nunca solos a la carretera del norte.

On the North Expressway

There's light over the slopes
on the North Expressway.
                      Ana, Amelia,
come with me to receive the light.

In my left hand I've got Amelia's hand,
and in my right one, Ana's.
The three of us feel our life and the light.
The three of us feel our hands and the light.
The three of us feel the light,
the silence, and the hands.

There was a day when I walked alone through the land.
Sun was still shining over the yellow slope
but loneliness blinded the light.

Even though there's sun shining, my friends,
never go alone to the North Expressway.

Un tren sobre la tierra

Voy en el tren hacia mi casa.

Los cabellos ásperos de mi madre
están rodeando su rostro sobre la almohada
y su viejo cuerpo ha caído en el sueño.

Cuando yo encienda la bombilla, ella
dará un grito de espanto y amor
y en la habitación habrá una gran luz amarilla
en la que viviremos abrazados.

Ahora voy en el tren
y en el departamento hay cuatro seres humanos.

Bajo el número cuarenta y cuatro,
una mujer hinchada de tristeza.

Bajo el número cuarenta y cinco,
un viejo arde en su mirada roja.

Bajo el número cuarenta y siete,
un hombre duerme con un gran capazo

La ventana es una lámina negra.
Vuelvo a mirar hacia mis compañeros:

La mujer respira dulcemente;
la respiración levanta su corazón tranquilo.

El viejo cierra la mirada y duerme.

El hombre desenvuelve un poco de fruta
y la mastica despacio.

A Train over the Land

I'm heading home on the train.

My mother's rough hair
is surrounding her face on the pillow
and her old body has fallen asleep.

When I turn on the light bulb, she'll
scream with fear and love
and we'll live embraced
in a great yellow light filling the room.

Now I'm riding the train
and there are four human beings in the compartment.

Under number forty-four,
a woman swollen with sadness.

Under number forty-five,
an old man burns in his red sight.

Under number forty-seven,
a man sleeps with a huge basket.

The window is a black sheet.
I look again at my companions:

The woman is very sweetly breathing;
air is coming out of her heart.

The old man closes his gaze and sleeps.

The man unwraps a bit of fruit
and chews it slowly.

Ahora estamos en paz en el departamento.
Yo me siento ir hacia mi casa
y cada uno siente que se aleja o que vuelve.

El tren avanza bajo la noche.
Vamos juntos atravesando la tierra.

Now we are in peace in the compartment.
I feel myself going home
and each one feels they're leaving or returning.

The train moves forward beneath the night.
We're crossing the land together.

Siento el agua

Me he sentado esta tarde a la orilla del río
mucho tiempo, quizá mucho tiempo,
hasta que mis ojos fluían con el agua
y mi piel era fresca como la piel del río.

Cuando llegó la noche, ya no veía el agua
pero la sentía descender en la sombra.
No escuchaba otro ruido que aquel ruido en la noche;
no sentía en mí más que el sonido del agua.

¡Tantos seres humanos, tan inmensa la tierra,
y este ruido en la noche ha bastado para llenar mi corazón!

Yo no sé si he traicionado a mis amigos:
el cántaro está lleno de un agua oscura y dulce,
pero el cántaro sufre —el rojo, viejo barro.

Alguien tiene piedad de este cántaro.
Alguien comprende el cántaro y el agua.
Alguien rompe su cántaro por amor.

En todo caso, yo no he cogido el agua
para bebérmela yo mismo.

I Feel the Water

I've sat this evening by the river shore
a long time, maybe a long time,
until my eyes flowed with the water
and my skin was as cool as the skin of the river.

When night came, I couldn't see the water anymore,
but I felt it descending in the shadow.
I didn't hear another noise but that noise in the night;
I didn't feel but the sound of the water in me.

So many humans, so immense the earth,
and this noise in the night was enough to fill my heart!

I don't know if I've betrayed my friends:
the jug is full of a dark and sweet water,
but the jug suffers —the red, old clay.

Someone pities this jug.
Someone understands the jug and the water.
Someone breaks his jug for love.

In any case, I did not take the water
to drink it myself.

La noche hasta caer

Toda la noche yo busqué sus ojos,
la mirada entre pieles, abrasada;
aquella lucidez excesiva.
Toda la noche hasta caer envuelto
en la mirada roja de mi amigo
y en la cobardía de mi corazón.

Íbamos de la noche a las tabernas
amarillas a cambiar el silencio
exterior por una voz fraterna
entre cuatro paredes y aquel vino
recio en la boca y frío en las entrañas:

"—¿Qué dices, viejo? Hablas sin cabeza.
¿Ahora lloras con los dientes?
                        —Calla.
Son las maderas húmedas, el frío
de los vasos, la ropa
gruesa de los trabajadores…"

(Era, toda la noche,
una certidumbre que volvía.)

"—Tú no tienes razón, pero la tienes
más que nada en el mundo.
                        —Bebe.
                        —Caes
al agujero de ti mismo.
                        —Caigo
sobre los brazos de mis camaradas".

Night until Falling

I sought his eyes throughout the night,
my gaze among skins, red and damp;
that excessive lucidity.
All night until falling down wrapped
in my friend's red sight
and in the cowardice of my heart.

We went from the night
to the yellow taverns to trade the outward
silence for a fraternal voice
amidst four walls, and that strong
wine in our mouth, and cold in our guts:

"—What say you, old man? You speak mindlessly.
Do you weep with your teeth now?
                              —Shut up.
There is damp lumber, the chill
of the glasses, the workers'
thick clothing..."

(All night, it was
a returning certainty.)

"—You're not right, but you are
more than anything in this world.
                         —Drink.
                         —You fall
into the hole of yourself.
                  —I fall
into my comrade's arms".

Recuerdo
un árbol blanco, alto, desnudo,
al otro lado de la carretera.
Me lo mostraba con sus manos:
                            "—Mira
mira ese árbol".
              No podía
hablar apenas, pero el árbol
se reunía con sus manos. Eran
una sola cosa en la noche:
un árbol y un hombre que se comprendían juntos.
Nada más. No voy a olvidarlo.

Íbamos de la noche a las tabernas
amarillas a olvidar el silencio.

Había una verdad, no se me olvide,
había una verdad.
                Dure la noche
y caiga yo a su misma tierra.

I recall
a tall, white naked tree
at the other side of the road.
He showed it to me with his hands:
                                        "—Look,
look at that tree".
                        He could barely
speak, but the tree
met with his hands. They
were the same thing in the night:
a tree and a man understanding each other.
Nothing else. I will not forget it.

We went from the night
to the yellow taverns to forget the silence.

There was a truth, I shouldn't forget,
there was a truth.
                        Should the night last
and should I fall to its same ground.

Después del accidente

Cuando levantaron aquel hierro amarillo,
se vio la cosa reventada: dos;
las dos manos del hombre: la gran mano
izquierda, la gran mano derecha.
Machacadas en óxido. La sangre
se espesó con el aire. Lo llevaron.

Si nos vemos, amigo, hay que beber a la salud del hierro.
Llevaré hasta tu boca el vaso con vino
y, cuando sientas que bebes con mis manos,
comprenderás que no estás manco en el mundo.

Yo te aseguro que cuando venga lo que ha de venir
nadie va a llorar por sus viejas manos atadas.

After the Accident

When they lifted that yellow iron,
we saw the burst thing: two;
both man's hands: the big left
hand, the big right hand.
Crushed in rust. The blood
thickened in the air. They took him.

If we see each other, my friend, we have to drink to the iron.
I'll bring the glass of wine to your mouth
and, when you feel that you are drinking with my hands,
you'll understand that you are not crippled in this world.

I assure you when what is to come comes
nobody is going to cry for his old tied hands.

Caigo sobre una silla

Cuando caigo sobre una silla y mi cabeza roza la muerte;
cuando cojo con mis manos la tiniebla de las cazuelas;
o cuando contemplo los documentos representativos de la tristeza,
es la amistad quien me sostiene.

I Fall on a Chair

When I fall on a chair, and my head brushes death;
when I grab the darkness of the pots with my hands;
or when I contemplate the documents representing the blues,
friendship is who holds me.

Your Words Matter

Your Words Matter

www.ingramcontent.com/pod-product-compliance
Lightning Source LLC
Chambersburg PA
CBHW030452010526
44118CB00011B/900